Keep your new teachers from running out the door
Designing new teacher induction programs

Dr. Catherine Turner

Copyright © 2020 Dr. Catherine Turner

Copyright © 2020 Generis Publishing

All rights reserved. This book or any portion thereof may not be reproduced or used in any manner whatsoever without the written permission of the publisher except for the use of brief quotations in a book review.

CIP a Camerei Naţionale a Cărţii

Turner, Catherine.

Keep your new teachers from running out the door : Designing new teacher induction programs / Dr. Catherine Turner. – Chişinău : Generis Publishing, 2020 (Print on demand). – 44 p.

Referinţe bibliogr.: p. 35-44.

ISBN 978-9975-153-19-5.

37.091

T 95

Cover image: www.pixabay.com

Generis Publishing
Online orders: www.generis-publishing.com
Orders by email: info@generis-publishing.com

Table of Contents

Chapter One 7
   Introduction and Background 7
   Definition of Terms 11
   Introduction Summary 13
Chapter Two 15
   Background 15
   Leave the profession 15
   Migrate 18
   Barriers 19
   Highly Qualified and Certification Expectations 22
   Culture and Climate 23
   Mentors 24
Chapter Three 27
   Theoretical Framework 27
Chapter Four 31
   Successful Teacher Induction Programs 31
References 35

Chapter One

Introduction and Background

Attrition of new teachers has held steady since the late 1980s in the United States (Bureau of Labor Statistics, 2018). A recession and the Gulf Wars did not impact new teachers leaving in their first three years in the profession (National Center for Education Statistics, 2016). The impact of the 2020 Covid Novel Virus is too early to determine. Teacher retirement accounted for less than a third of teachers that left the profession in recent years (Ingersoll, Merrill, Stuckey, and Collins, 2018). Older people joined the profession in 2015-16 where 42% were 29 or older and 19% were 40 and over. Women significantly joined the profession more than men in 1988 to 2016 percentage-wise (BLS, 2018). The number of men did not decline, rather, the need for more teachers increased with mandated smaller class sizes, increased state math and science requirement classes for graduation, least restrictive classroom mandates, and higher demand in school districts for inclusion special education teachers. The United States hired more teachers from 1988 to 2016 and more were women (Ingersoll, et al, 2018). Schools and Staffing Survey (SASS) by the National Center for Education Statistics (NCES) state that new teachers continue to leave the profession within the first three years (2016).

Ingersoll's academic team (2016) found that teacher effectiveness as measured by student academic achievement on standardized test scores greatly increased with experience in the first several years of teaching (Fortner and Bastian,, 2012). Research supports that often the higher quality and brighter educators are the first to leave teaching (Classroom Ideas That Work, 2007). Over 40 school districts in Georgia implemented new teacher induction programs from 2010 to the present, providing opportunities to ascertain the efficacy of the program components and provide a framework to design an optimal new teacher induction program. (Turner, 2015). One of the strongest ways to increase student academics is to develop skills and experience in novice teachers (Working Conditions Key for Teacher Retention, R&D Alert, 2005). Prepared teacher programs such as an induction program are aligned directly with student academic achievement (Darling-Hammond, 1999). The quality of teaching is the single greatest impact on student academic achievement (Edwards, 2008). Russell found that higher student achievements were measured with novice teachers that completed an induction program (2006). Induction programs help develop new teachers into veteran, master teachers (Turner, 2015).

Brand new teachers, so new they sparkle, are vulnerable to three big issues: the workload, certification requirements, and expectations under government policy and legislation, and the lack of support by leadership (Turner, 2015). No Child Left Behind along with other legislation requirements contributes to new teacher burnout as enthusiasm and passion are often buried under standardized testing expectations and paperwork (Kopkowski, 2008). Recent education graduates have strong theoretical knowledge in hand with some student teaching experience gained under the supervision of a veteran teacher assigned by the college. However, actual practice in classroom management and other best practices are gained by experience in leading a classroom. New teachers often despair with disillusionment in their first year of teaching without skills that may only be acquired in the actual practice over time (Long, 2004).

Adequate Yearly Progress (AYP) standards have escalated the stress for new teachers as consequences for schools, students, and stakeholders are significant. Lower performing schools that fail to meet AYP standards for three consecutive years have heavy penalties including replacing the entire teaching staff and administration in some states as well as student options to transfer schools (No Child Left Behind, 2002). Failing the AYP for two consecutive years garners negative media attention and destroys the morale of communities, teachers, and students (Blagojevich, 2007). Federal and state funds may be reduced and schools can be forced to provide tutors and other services beyond the normal school day at no additional cost to the student. Keeping effective new teachers has never been more important in the current high stakes environment.

Turner's study (2015) analyzed the effectiveness of components of Georgia's new teacher induction programs to determine the relevancy of the specific components in retaining new teachers. The research supported that new teacher induction programs are critical to providing the safety net, encouragement, and professional development to retain teachers and to keep new teachers satisfied with their work (Alliance for Excellent Education, 2004; Capelluti and Nye, 2002; Carver, 2002; Cooke, 2007; Ganser, 2002; Turner, 2015; and Wynn, 2006). Replacing new teachers continuously costs time, money, and effort and impacts the school environment and stakeholders (Guinn, 2004).

Research supports that there is a wide range of what teachers require to feel successful in teacher induction programs (Turner, 2015). Just as students all have different learning styles, teachers require different aspects of induction programs. New teachers come in several different varieties, age, race, experience among other variables. Not all require the same support. New and veteran teachers new to a building or district have significantly different perceptions in their own feelings of efficacy with relation to components of new teacher induction programs in Georgia (Turner, 2015). In addition, variables that impact the retention of new teachers in their current position include salary, genders, tenure, years of experience, age, and the curriculum taught. For example, science and math are more likely to return to work in any industry than other academic teachers (Ingersoll, et al 2018). Research suggests that conflicting data is available as to the efficacy of new teacher induction programs (Wong, 2002). Some components worked well and some did not and often in the same district in different buildings (Turner, 2015).

The U.S. Department of Education commissioned a study with the Education Commission of the State to study teacher recruitment and retention (Eight Questions, 2007). NInety-one studies in the composite study identified successful components of a successful induction and mentoring program. Control groups with no mentoring or induction were included in only three of these studies. Turner (2015) included a control group that predated the new teacher induction programs prior to 2009 which supported that teachers who participated in a new teacher induction program were more likely to choose to retain their position after their first year of teaching than teachers who did not participate in a new teacher induction program.

Definition of Terms

Attrition is defined as the situation where the teacher completely leaves the profession of education and not transfers to another school (Norton, 1999).

Climate describes the tangible, predictable, and measurable components in a school building or system that impacts the stakeholders (Lucksinger, 2000).

Culture is the oft undefinable, intangible events, stories, relationships and history of a school environment that is often not easily identified or discernable (Marshall, 2006; Owens, 2004).

Demographics are independent variables that do not change such as a teacher's age, gender, certifications, or enure (Gall, 2007; Wynn, 2006).

Fiscal Compensation is the total benefits and salary package provided within one contract year for a teacher (NCES, 1997).

IEP is an individual education plan for a student that is designed by a committee including teachers, administration, counselors, and guardians and specifically details the supports and resources available for that student as well as expectations for growth by that specific student (U.S. Department of Education, 2010).

Induction defines any program no matter how complex that provides any resources or support for new teachers including but not limited to mentoring, positive learning communities, and individual professional development (Kaufman, 2007: Mentoring Programs, 2002; Turner, 2015).

Least Restrictive Environment is the legal requirement for a student to be educated with his peers in general education to the maximum extent possible (U.S. Department of Education, 2010).

Mentor is a master teacher that formally or informally supports a new teacher (Bolich, 2000; Jorissen, 2002).

Migration is the situation where a teacher, new or veteran, transfers from one school building to another, changes teaching content, returns to college for advanced degrees full time with the intention of returning to the profession or changes position while staying in education (Claycomb, 1998; Norton, 1999)

Novice or new teacher is a brand new, first-year teacher (Norton, 1999).

Retention is the situation where a teacher stays in the same classroom, the same building teaching the same course and grade, from one school year to the next (Norton, 1999).

Veteran teachers have at least one year of experience (Norton, 1999). Turner's study (2015) supports that teachers consider themselves veteran teachers after the third year of teaching the same subject to the same grade level. The third year mark for self-perception as a veteran is backed up by research that found that teachers with three or more years of teaching experience are more effective than novice teachers with only one of two years experience (Clotfelter, Ladd & Vigdor, 2007).

Introduction Summary

The strongest teacher induction programs start at the interview to identify highly qualified and interested candidates (Clement, 2002). Aligning novice teachers with areas of their expertise and interest as well as mentors in the same content area improve the chances of retaining them. They are more comfortable and have a better chance of impacting their strong knowledge to their students. The greatest preventable loss for teachers leaving the profession happens in the first five years (School and Staffing survey, 2012). Novice teachers who scored in the top 25% of ACT or SAT national assessment tests leave more than the rest (Edwards, 2008).

Chapter Two

Background

The big question is how do school districts retain novice K-12 public school teachers? This complex issue as stated in Chapter One is unique for each novice teacher. However, there are a few common key issues to consider. Why do teachers leave and why do teachers migrate positions? What are the barriers for teachers to stay in their position? What impact do highly qualified certification expectations have on novice teachers? How do workplace conditions such as administration, culture and climate, and physical environment impact novice teachers' decision to stay? Do mentors matter in induction programs? Do teachers leave or migrate based on their personal demographics?

Leave the profession

Teachers leave the profession within the first five years of teaching. As many as 39% leave in the first five years (Bolich, 2000; Heller, 2004; Cornett and Gaines, 2002, Ingersoll et. al, 2018, Turner, 2015). They fought for their degree, acquired student loans, student taught, passed stringent competency, and curriculum-based tests. These novice teachers each work one to five years and leave to face the consequences of unforgiven student loans and other issues.

Annual costs for the United States for novice teacher attrition has been estimated in excess of seven billion dollars (NCTAF, 2007). Retaining novice teachers to gain experience to move from confusion to competence is a high priority and critical to maintaining school and state fiscal balances. Research supports that experienced teachers who are highly qualified, skilled, knowledgeable, caring, and culturally astute have students who reach their greatest academic achievements (Berry, 2004). The brain drain of emerging experienced teachers is making it difficult for school districts to place a highly qualified teacher in every classroom as mandated by federal law (NCLB, 2002). Ingersoll (2002) found that the most highly qualified novice teachers are more likely to be the ones that leave in the first five years. Statistically, the novice teacher who leaves was in the top of their class and a high achiever (Edwards, 2008), in an urban school, in a minority or a low-income educational environment, and in a classroom that outside knowledge comfort levels (Metlife, 2006) and no teacher induction or mentor (Turner, 2015).

In no particular order, novice teachers leave the profession for a combination of reasons. Recognizing the reasons and addressing as many as possible in a new teacher induction program will assist retention.

1. Novice teachers burn out from the stress of classroom management (Fredricks, 2005). Student behavior is disrespectful and even dangerous. Novice teachers lack training and experience in classroom management techniques.

2. New teachers without mentors and other peer interactions are often lonely and feel isolated (Walters, 2004). Collaboration is often missing with no sense of belonging (Geert Kelchtermans, 2017). A 2004 poll (Governor Easley's Teacher Working Conditions Initiatie in North Carolina) found that 34% of novice teachers stayed because they felt valued and were not isolated with a supportive collegial atmosphere.

3. Student academic achievement solely resides with the teacher with very little accountability required of other stakeholders (American Federation of Teachers, 2015).

4. Students appear to not care about high stakes testing, critical to the individual teacher and Adequate Yearly Progress as required by NCLB and federal funding (Fredricks, 2005).

5. Novice teachers are expected to have the same responsibilities as veteran teachers and often are given the least desirable classes as well as coaching and sponsorship expectations that lead to stress and burnout (Turner, 2015). In addition, apart from mentors, few veteran teachers assist novice teachers in these responsibilities.

6. Full responsibilities and expectations about classroom management, outside instruction responsibilities and extracurricular activities are not explained clearly in the job interview, leading to frustration with novice teachers (Osgood and Self, 2003). Research supports the failure to inform applicants during the job interview process about additional duties outside the classroom lead to teacher attrition (Richin, Banyon, Stein, and Banyon, 2003).

7. Minimal, one-year induction historically has shown no discernible difference with new teachers with no induction programs (Classroom ideas that work, 2007).

8. Administrators are not encouraging and supportive, only critical in the few interactions with novice teachers (Frericks, 2005).

9. Compensation is not comparable to what is offered in industry for similar positions (MetLife, 2006).

10. Mentors are not trained and the better, more experienced veteran teachers often do not mentor (Osgood and Self, 2003).

These factors and other barriers impact the overall attitude of the novice teacher and the decision to remain in the same position that second and third year (Fredericks, 2005; Turner, 2015).

Migrate

Novice teachers often stay in the profession yet change buildings or school districts, still causing a brain drain and the loss of a developing veteran, master teacher (MetLife, 2006; SASS 2006). In 2006, moving closer to home (26.2%), job security (19.1%) and improved salary and benefits (16.5%) were given as reasons for migration (SASS).

Barriers

One of the barriers for new teachers is that it is the only professional profession that expects the same performance level from first-year practitioners as seasoned teachers (Danielson and McGreat, 2000). Novice teachers often feel confused and lacking with the tasks and challenges expected (Berry, 2004). Expectations continue to increase due to LRE and IEP expectations as well, adding to the stress for novice teachers. Another barrier for novice teachers occurs when their peer novice teachers migrate or leave the profession (Guinn, 2004). Chronic teacher turnover impacts climate, culture, and school functionality and serves as a strong indicator of a school with problems.

Novice teachers that remain often see others successfully navigating a new career in industry and leave the following year. When any teacher leaves, staff development and recruitment time and spent energy is a lost resource. Those teachers who stay often have lower morale and develop trust issues with their peers. In a high turn-over educational environment, teamwork is difficult because time is precious and lost when peer teachers leave (Turner, 2015).

Another barrier is projections showing an enrollment increase for public school students to 2025 to increase 2% from 2013 numbers or about 0.7 million students. To serve all students in public schools elementary and secondary, projections show that teacher requirements increase by 6% or about a quarter of a million new teachers. With a leaky bucket of new teacher attrition and a need for more teachers by 2025, the education profession is facing a projected shortage of teachers. Teachers without veteran teachers in the hall to support them are often vulnerable and feel distressed.

A 2015 study of 30,000 teachers found that over 75% reported that work is stressful (American Federation of Teachers). Positive teacher experiences are related to better student achievement, with the greatest impact occurring during the first five years of teaching (Clotfelter, Ladd, & Vigdor, 2007). Browser and Tomic (2000) found that novice teachers are very positive, open to feedback and eager to develop effective practices. An ineffective induction program will negatively impact enthusiasm. Veteran teachers who are new to a school system have the barrier that established approaches are already set and may be less likely to be receptive to habits of practice (Harmsen 35 al., 2018).

MetLife (2006) surveyed novice teachers who left the profession in the first three years. Several reasons were given including a lack of resources in the classroom. For example, some had no textbooks in the classroom. Classroom equipment was antiquated. School buildings and classrooms were debilitated and not clean.

A main barrier that caused teachers to leave included 40% that felt personal frustration of having no influence on decisions made in their own classroom (MetLife, 2006). The perception of no participation and input in classroom and educational decisions was disheartening (Turner, 2015). In addition, novice teachers became frustrated with activities and responsibilities that took valuable planning, preparation and grading time during their scheduled planning time. Few industries expect a beginning employee to perform at the same level with the same job responsibilities as veterans (Stausburg, 2002).

Low salaries and poor administration support distress new teachers and create barriers to stay in the profession (Ingersoll, 2000). Every year, more paperwork seems to be pushed onto teachers through building, administration, and district expectations. New teachers often feel overwhelmed with the paperwork involved with teaching (Carver, 2002; Norton, 1999).

A common lament is that the general lack of support in the communities for teaching as a profession is discouraging (Zeichner, 2003). Norton (1999) research indicates that low salaries create financial problems for novice teachers, requiring many to take second and third jobs that impact physical stamina and distract novice teachers.

There are several barriers for new teachers that include minimal personal prestige in communities, low salaries and benefits, minimal control over the classroom, few resources for diverse learners, unappreciative principals, distress, classroom misbehavior and early burn-out (American Federation of Teachers, 2015; MetLife, 2006; Turner, 2015; and Zeichner, 2003). New teachers are challenged by increasing accountability on their part, and increasing paperwork (Working Conditions Key for Teacher Retention, R&D Alert, 2005). Classroom demands exceed resources for novice teachers, leading to increased stress and the greater likelihood of leaving the teaching profession (McCarthy, Fitchett, Lambert & Boyle, 2019). The top reason teachers left in the MetLife study (2006) was the distress of feeling personally unqualified to teach the curriculum. Teachers are hired into content areas they may be qualified on paper for yet lack the ability to scaffold existing knowledge to a new content area.

Highly Qualified and Certification Expectations

Highly qualified educators matter. Multiple research studies across several states and countries confirms that teacher qualifications directly impact student learning (Cardichon, Darling-Hammond, Yang,, Scott, Shields, & Burns (2020). Anderson (2020) found that students of highly qualified novice teachers significantly outperformed students of not highly qualified novice teachers. Wright (2020) compared Arkansas pedagogical knowledge of novice teachers from traditional and alternative certification paths. Her findings were no discernable difference. Expectations are that novice teachers are now highly qualified and certified in their subject area (Turner, 2015). Lynch (2000) recommends a minimum of a bachelor's degree for all career and technical secondary education teachers. This study suggested increased and supported certification requirements through a strong induction program.

No Child Left Behind (2002) and other federal and state legislation required additional standardized testing expectations for teacher evaluations, school district funding and other stick and carrot type punishments and rewards (Turner, 2015). Not new for teachers, Shaker found that novice teachers were distressed by high expectations for student academic performances to show content mastery without any consideration for individual diverse students, culture and climate, nature abilities, and student interest (1996). In addition to highly qualified certifications, professional development that flooded novice teachers with new technology, best practices, and expectations led to increased distress and attrition (School and staffing survey, 2006; Turner, 2015).

Administration

New teacher induction programs work best when administration is fully invested in the program, supporting new teachers, and providing immediate feedback and positive reinforcement (Kutsyuruba & Walker, 2020; Turner, 2015). Administration is critical to retain novice teachers as supported by a North Carolina poll where 27% of teachers stayed mainly because of the strong, instructional emphasis of the Principal (Governor Easley's Teacher Working Conditions Initiative in North Carolina, 2004). Administration that supported new teachers including resources and protected times for planning retained novice teachers at higher rates. Also, teachers were personally empowered to make impactful decisions in their classroom. In fact, demographics such as race, gender, advanced degrees, types of certification, and experience altogether were found to be less important for retention than the support of strong, positive administrators. In scheduling, often the most behaviorally challenging classes and groups are given to the newer teachers.

Culture and Climate

NCES (School and Staffing Survey, 2011, National Teacher and Principal Survey, 2018) surveys factors that impact climate and culture in schools including workplace conditions, class size, safety, teacher autonomy, and isolation. Consistently from the 1993 report to current results, favorable, positive working conditions and perceived job satisfaction are more important to retaining novice teachers than any other variable. School climate is measurable as the physical structure of the building and the interactions between all stakeholders such as teachers, parents/guardians, and staff (Marshal, 2006). Culture is not easily measured as it is impacted by diversity and demographics of all stakeholders and has an immediate change when there is a change such as a tragedy, schedule change, or an external event such as the Covid virus (Gideon, 2002; McBrien and Brandt, 1997; Marshall, 2006). A successful school culture has strong, positive relationships between administration and teachers (Glickman, 2002). Owens (2004) found that the culture in every school is unique as the history and stakeholders are unique. Veteran teachers who transfer buildings have to decipher behavior norms, values, traditions, rituals, stories and myths, relationships and history. Human nature is complex. The effectiveness of student academic achievement is rooted in the quality of positive school culture (Owens, 2004).

Mentors

Odysseus prepared to travel and left his young son, Telemachus, to the care of his trust friend, Mentor (Homer, trans. 1968). Mentor had full authority over the household to raise Telemachus and keep him safe. A mentor watches over a new teacher and helps raise them into a veteran, confident, successful teacher.

Research supports that the better mentors are in the same content area and similar grade levels (Jorissen, 2002). Similar demographics, knowledge about the content area, communicative, experienced, and the same gender all make a strong mentor. Ideally, mentors support only one new teacher in an academic year and provide positive feedback and authentic assessments in a non-threatening way on a regular basis (Danielson and McGreat, 2000; Jorrisen, 2002; Turner, 2015). Orland-Barak and Wang (2020) support mentors in the field as early as during student teaching for the best results.

California started mentoring in the early 1990s after losing approximately 50% of new teachers annually (States hopeful that mentoring will retain new teachers, 2007). Mentoring is more powerful when combined with common planning and collaboration time (Ingersoll, 2004). A barrier is often that veteran teachers do not care to mentor. Mentors may be compensated for their extra effort and time by in-service credits, stipends, or reduction of teachers outside of the classroom responsibilities (Turner, 2015). Ideally, mentors receive professional development in how to support new teachers, have multiple communication opportunities including common planning, both novice and mentor teachers are released from extra duties, team teaching is allowed, and a positive, non-judgemental relationship is developed (Barnett, 1995; Bey, 1992; Edwards, 2008; Ingersoll, 2004; Jorissen, 2002; Stedman, 2003; Wong, 2002).

Chapter Three

Theoretical Framework

Turner's study (2015) supported rooting an induction program in four critical elements of learning: motivation, reinforcement, retention of knowledge and transference (Lieb, 1991). Her study built on the work of Kowles (1990) and identified the following components in building an induction program. Stenger (2017) also recommended similar ways for adults to improve their transference of learning.

1. Novice teachers understand the relevancy of their own induction program and are involved in projects that reflect their interests (motivation).

2. Novice teachers bring a lifetime of learning, skills and experiences that may be generalized and scaffolded into classroom instruction (transference).

3. Novice teachers require clear goals and objectives (transference).

4. Novice teachers have gaps in knowledge that need identification and resources and time for self-explanation, self-examination and reflection (retention).

5. Novice teachers understand that knowledge and memory is often context dependent and benefit from role play to tie college knowledge to classroom execution to build self confidence (retention).

6. Novice teachers require respect from peers, mentors and administration to meet their human needs (motivation).

Humanistic theories such as Maslow (Benthan, 2002) supports that intrinsic motivation happens once all basic human needs are met. Positive reinforcement in an environment of praises and rewards creates an environment of educational achievement (Skinner, 1984). While the pay is not competitive for similar professions, there is financial security in teaching with annual contracts that meets the need for financial security. Collaboration and mentoring in induction programs meet the novice teacher's need for belonging and socialization. Teaching novice teachers to transfer book knowledge into practical knowledge is a critical component in induction (Skinner, 1981).

Social cognitive theory supports that believing a teacher induction program on the part of all stakeholders may guarantee the program works because stakeholders are invested and support the program (Gall, 2007). Perception becomes reality as stakeholders believe in the induction program. Hence, positivity and assuredness are critical when presenting the induction program to new teachers.

Six components that motivate people in the educational work environment include (Turner, 2015):

1. Continuous and immediate feedback and reinforcement from peers, mentors and administration.

2. Positive feedback and reinforcement from peers, mentors, and administration.

3. Small steps with clear goals and objectives.

4. Tackle the simple tasks and gradually progress to more complex.

5. Scaffold specialty knowledge into more general knowledge.

6. Repeat directions as often as required to reinforce (Kolb, 1984).

When novice teachers feel safe, free from the threat of any physical or emotional harm, the best academic environment occurs (Lezotte, 1991). Novice teachers are retained historically when clear goals and objectives are provided with immediate and relevant feedback (Knowles, 1990; Lieb, 1991). Stenger's blog (2017) addresses ways to improve the transfer of learning from college to the work environment. Memory is triggered in context dependent induction programs. Novice teachers apply college knowledge to the classroom practice. Work is relevant and novice teachers have time to reflect on their lesson plans and classes. Gaps in knowledge are identified and supported with resources. Clear goals are provided. Novice teachers are shown how to scaffold existing knowledge as well as generalize their specialized knowledge. Collaborative opportunities, analogies and metaphors are provided. Ideally, all lower level basic human needs are met by the teaching position on Maslow's hierarchy of needs pyramid (Bentham, 2002). The theoretical framework for designing a new teacher induction program appears to work best when it is rooted in solid instructional design and adult learning principles that address four critical elements of learning: motivation, reinforcement, retention, and transference (Jarvis, 1995; Knowles, 1990; Kolb and Kolb, 2006; Lieb, 1995, Turner, 2015).

Chapter Four

Successful Teacher Induction Programs

Practices that grow novice teachers into competent and effective professionals with effective skills are recommended for inclusion in teacher induction programs (APEC Teacher Induction Study, 1997). Common goals for several teacher induction programs researched include improving everyday novice teacher performance, increasing the retention of novice teachers in the same position with attrition or migration, providing the emotional, mental and physical support for the overall well-being of novice teachers, and meeting all legally mandated requirements including special education, certification, and professional development (Turner, 2015). A well-designed teacher induction program reduces new teacher attrition (Brighton, 2000) and transitions the new teacher from being the *new kid on the block* to being *one of the guys* (Ingersoll, 2000).

Ingersoll and Smith (2004) found a strong positive correlation between new teacher induction programs and novice teacher attrition. Successful induction programs contain a myriad of support where teachers could pick and choose their resources with the sole exception of a mentor that is mandatory. One common theme from research is a strong need for administration involvement in induction (Carver, 2002).

There are several different things that administration can do to assist novice teachers and reduce attrition. Release the new teacher and the mentor teacher from extracurricular activities outside the classroom (Wong, 2002). Allow common planning time for the mentor and novice teacher and opportunities for the two to team teach. One observed scenario had the Assistant Principal teach the mentor class once a month to allow the mentor to join the novice teacher in the classroom. Norton (1999) found that authentic, positive assessment and constructive, immediate feedback improved the morale of novice teachers. Effective, formal training on evaluations for administration developed new teacher confidence and skills (Edwards, 2008; Glickman, 2002). Behavior challenging students distributed evenly among classrooms keeps new teachers from receiving a disproportionate level of "trouble-makers" (Carver, 2002; Turner, 2015). Administration may provide clerical help with paperwork or reduce the amount of required paperwork for new teachers (Guinn, 2004).

The APEC Study found that effective induction programs all contained some instruction in various teaching methodologies, in dissecting standards and curriculum content, in classroom management techniques with role-play scenarios, in safely advising and counseling students, and in navigating school politics (1997). When effective teaching strategies and techniques were role played or modeled to new teachers, one study found new teacher retention jumped 21% over three years (Elli, 2008). Alliance for Excellent Education (2004) expects a positive relationship between new teachers and stakeholders as an outcome from an effective induction program.

Best practices of induction (2002) reviewed 225 public school districts and found nine common components shared by successful programs:

1. A minimum of five days orientation that included culture and climate about the building and district.

2. Standards and curriculum review.

3. Lower ratio of student to teacher than veteran teachers.

4. No outside duty responsibilities.

5. Introduction during orientation and time throughout the school year with mentor teacher through common planning.

6. Observation of best practices modeled by veteran teachers.

7. Opportunity to give and receive timely, positive feedback.

8. Adequate materials and supplies for the classroom.

9. On-going professional development.

The most successful new teacher induction programs support new teachers with leadership coaching, reduced workload expectations, and support with paperwork from mentors (Turner, 2015). New teachers do not spend precious time trying to figure out technology because induction trained them on every software and equipment used by the district. Information about the school's culture and climate are embedded into the teacher induction program which decreases feelings of isolation and increases buy-in into the school, increasing retention of new teachers (Ganswer, 2002; Owens, 2004;

Wynn, 2006). Turner (2015) found that mentors work best when matched with new teachers based on strengths, common curriculum and grade levels, older and veteran teachers as mentors, and there is some compensation for mentor time and effort (Best practices in induction, 2002; Jorissen, 2002). Professional development works best when it is meaningful and applicable for the grade level, curriculum, and standards. Modeling and role-play of classroom management techniques raise the comfort level of new teachers in their classroom. Coping mechanisms modeled in orientation help new teachers emotionally. Documentation of teacher strengths encourage and build confidence. New teachers to the building, even if veteran teachers, require induction because climate and culture vary greatly.

References

Alliance for Excellent Education, (2004). *Tapping the potential: Retaining and developing high-quality new teachers.* Ishington, DC: Authorhouse.

American Federation of Teachers, 2015. Quality of worklife survey. https://www.aft.org/sites/default/files/worklifesurveyresults2015.pdf

Anderson, K. A. (2020). A National Study of the Differential Impact of Novice Teacher Certification on Teacher Traits and Race-Based Mathematics Achievement. Journal of Teacher Education, 71(2), 247–260. https://doi.org/10.1177/0022487119849564

Barnett, B.G. (1995). Developing reflection and expertise: Can mentors make the difference? Journal of Educational Administration, 33(5), 45-49.

Bentham, s. (2002). *Psychology and Education.* Hove, East Sussex: UK: Routledge.

Berry, B. (2002). Recruiting and retaining "highly qualified teachers" for hard-to-staff schools. NASSP Bulletin 88, 5-27.

Bolich, A.M. (2000). Reduce your losses: Help new teachers become veteran teachers, Atlanta, GA: Southern Regional Education Board: 14.

Brighton, E. et al. (2000). More swimming, less sinking: perspectives on teacher induction in the U.S. and abroad. National Center for improving education, West Ed: 17.

Bureau of Labor Statistics. (2018). Labor Force Statistics from the Current Population Survey https://www.bls. gov/cps/cpsaat11.htm

Capelluti, J. & Nye, K. (2002). Now you see me, now you didn't. *Principal Leadership.* 3(1). National Association of Secondary shcool Principals.

Cardichon, J., Darling-Hammond, L., Yang, M., Scott, C., Shields, P. M., & Burns, D. (2020). Inequitable opportunity to learn: Student access to certified and experienced teachers. Palo Alto, CA: Learning Policy Institute.

Carver, C. L. (2002). *Principal's supporting role in new teacher induction.* Doctoral dissertation, Michigan State University, East Lansing.

Christopher J. McCarthy, Paul G. Fitchett, Richard G. Lambert & Lauren Boyle (2019) Stress vulnerability in the first year of teaching, Teaching Education, DOI: 10.1080/10476210.2019.1635108

Claycomb, C. (2000). High-quality urban school teachers: What they need to enter and to remain in hard-to-staff schools. *The State Education Standard,* 1(1), 17–21.

Clement, Mary (2002, September). *Help wanted: How to hire the best teachers*. Principal Leadership High School Edition.

Clotfelter, C. T., Ladd, H. F., & Vigdor, J. L. (2007). How and why do teacher credentials matter for student achievement? (NBER Working Paper 12828). Cambridge, MA: National Bureau of Economic Research; Kini,

T., & Podolsky, A. (2016). Does teaching experience increase teacher effectiveness? A review of the research. Palo Alto, CA: Learning Policy Institute. https://learningpolicyinstitute.org/product/ does-teaching-experience-increase-teacher-effectiveness-review-research.

Cooke, C. (2007, June 21). Turnover in teachers is called 'out of control.' *Chattanooga Times Free Press*.

Creswell, J. W. (2003). *Research design: Qualitative, quantitative, and mixed methods approaches* (2nd ed.). Thousand Oaks, CA: Sage Publications.

Danielson, C. & McGreat, T. (2000). Teacher Evaluation to enhance professional practice. Alexandria, VA: Association for Supervision and Curriculum Development.

Edwards, V.B. (2008). Quality counts 2008: A new framework for strengthening the teaching profession. Retrieved February 18, 2008 from

Http://www.edweek.org/media/ew/qc/2008/QC08PressPacketFINALcompressed.pdf

Eight Questions on teacher recruitment and retention: what does the research say? Education Commission of the Stated. Retrieved July 9, 2007 from http://www.ecs.org/html/educationissues/teachingquality/trrreport/chapters/07/researchsays.asp.

Fredricks, J. (2005, April 26). Why teachers leave. *Education Digest.*

Gall, M., Gall, J., & Borg, W. *Educational research – an introduction.* (2007). (8th Ed.) Boston, MA: Pearson. p.32.

Ganser, T. (2002, September). Getting the MOST out of new-teacher mentoring programs. *Principal Leadership High School Edition.* National Association of Secondary School Principals.

Geert Kelchtermans (2017) 'Should I stay or should I go?': unpacking teacher attrition/retention as an educational issue, Teachers and Teaching, 23:8, 961-977, DOI: 10.1080/13540602.2017.1379793

Gideon, B. (2002, September). Supporting a collaborative culture. *Principal Leadership.*

Glickman, C. (2002). *Leadership for learning: How to help teachers succeed.* Alexandria, VA: Association for Supervision and Curriculum Development.

Governor Easley's teacher working conditions initiative in North Carolina (2004). Retrieved on February 6, 2007 from http://www.teachingquality.org/pdfs/twcsummary.pdf.

Guinn, K. (2004, August 16). *Chronic teacher turnover in urban elementary schools*, Education Policy Analysis Archives 12 (42) Retrieved on February 1, 2007 from http://epag.asu.edu/epaa/v12n42/v12n42.pdf.

Henry, G., Fortner, K., & Bastian, K. (2012). The effects of experience and attrition for novice high school science and mathematics teachers. Science, 335, 1118–1121.

Homer. *Odyssey*. (Trans. 1968). Retrieved on September 8, 2007 from http://classics.mit.edu/Homer/odyssey.2.ii.html.

Ingersoll, R.M. (2000). Turnover among mathematics and science teachers in the U.S. National Commission on Mathematics and Science Teaching for the 21st Century.

Ingersoll, R., Merrill, E., Stuckey, D., & Collins, G. (2018). Seven Trends: The Transformation of the Teaching Force, updated in October 2018. Research Report (#RR 2018–2). Consortium for Policy Research in Education, University of Pennsylvania.

Jarvis, P. (1995) *Adult and Continuing Education. Theory and practice* 2e, London: Routledge.

Jorissen, L., (2002, September). 10 Things a principal can did to retain teachers. *Principal Leadership.*

Kaufman, J. (2007). Teaching quality/induction programs and mentoring. Education Commission of the stated. Retrieved February 18, 2008 from http://www.ecs.org/clearinghouse/76/63/7663.pdf

Knowles, M. S. (1990). *The adult learner: A neglected species.* Houston: Gulf Publishing Company.

Kopkowski, C. (2008). Why they leave. *NEA Today. February, 2008.*

Kutsyuruba, B. & Walker, K. The Role of School Administrators in the Induction and Mentoring of Early Career Teachers . Online Publication Date: Apr 2020 https://oxfordre.com/education/view/10.1093/acrefore/9780190264093.001.0001/acrefore-9780190264093-e-659#acrefore-9780190264093-e-659-bibliography-0001

Lezotte, L. (1997). *Learning for all.* Okemos, MI: Effective School Products.

Lieb, S. (1991). Principles of adult learning. Retrieved October 1, 2006, from http://www.honolulu.hawaii.edu/intranet/committees/FacDevCom/guidebk/teachtip/adults-2.htm

Lindsay Joseph Wexler (2020) 'I would be a completely different teacher if I had been with a different mentor': Ways in which educative mentoring matters as novices learn to teach, Professional Development in Education, 46:2, 211-228, DOI: 10.1080/19415257.2019.1573375

Long, S. (2004, March). Separating rhetoric from reality: Supporting teachers in negotiating beyond the status quo. *Journal of Teacher Education.*

Lucksinger, L.N. (2000). Teachers: Can we get them and keep them? The Delta Kappa Gamma Bulletin: 11-15.

Lynch, R.L. (2000) High school career and technical education for the first decade of the 21st Century. *Journal of Vocational Education Research.* 25(2).

Marshall, M. (2006) *Examining school climate: defining factors and educational influences.* Retrieved February 2, 2007 from http://education.gsu.edu/schoolsafety/didwnload$20files/SWP%202002?20school%20climate.pdf.

McBrien, J.L. & Brandt (1997), R.S. *The language of learning: a guide to education terms.* Alexandria, VA: Association for Supervision and Curriculum Development.

No Child Left Behind Act of 2001, Pub. L. No. 107-110, § 103-104, 115 Stat. 1425 (2002).

Norton, M.S. (1999). Teacher retention: Reducing costly teacher turnover. Contemporary Education 70(3): 52-55

Orland-Barak, L., & Wang, J. (2020). Teacher Mentoring in Service of Preservice Teachers' Learning to Teach: Conceptual Bases, Characteristics, and Challenges for Teacher Education Reform. Journal of Teacher Education. https://doi.org/10.1177/0022487119894230

Osgood, V. & Self, M. (2003). Pathway to survival: A new teacher induction initiative. *Workforce Education Forum.*

Owens, R. (2004). *Organizational behavior in education – adaptive leadership and school reform.* (8th Ed.). Boston: Pearson.

Projections of Education Statistics to 2025/ National Center for Educational Statistics https://nces.ed.gov/pubs2017/2017019.pdf

Richin, R. Banyon, R., Stein, R. & Banyon, F. (2003). *Induction – connecting teacher recruitment to retention.* Thousand Oaks, CA: Corwin Press, 5.

Russell, A. (2006). Teacher Induction Programs: Trends and Opportunities. American Association of Colleges and Universities. Volume 3. Number 10. October 2006. Retrieved February 18, 2008 from http://www.aascu.org/policy_matters/pdf/v3n10.pdf

Schools and staffing survey (SASS) Overview (2006). Retrieved February 21, 2007 from http://nces.ed.gov/surveys/sass/.

Skinner, B.F. (1984, September). The shame of American education. *American Psychologist.* 39(9), 947-954.

Stausburg, K. & Zimmerman, J. (2002, Fall). Smart induction programs. *Journal of Staff Development.* 23(4). Retrieved September 8, 2007 from http://www.nsdc.org/library/publications/jsd/stausburg234.cfm.

Stedman, J. (2003). Induction – Connecting Teacher Recruitment to Retention. Thousand Oaks, CA: Corwin Press, Inc.

Stenger, M. (2017, May 11). 10 Ways to Improve Transfer of Learning. *informED. https://www.opencolleges.edu.au/informed/features/10-ways-improve-transfer-learning/*

U.S. Department of Education. (2010). Thirty-five Years of Progress in Educating Children With Disabilities Through IDEA. Retrieved from http://www2.ed.gov/about/offices/list/osers/idea35/history/idea-35-history.pdf

Walters, H. (2004). Why teachers leave the profession. *Delta Kappa Gamma Bulletin*, Fall 2004, 71(1), 58-60.

Wong, H. (2002). Play for keeps. *Principal Leadership.* 3 (1). Reston, VA: National Association of Secondary School Principals.

Wright, Karen (2020) "Comparison of Pedagogical Knowledge of Traditional and Alternate Routes to Teacher Certification," Journal of Graduate

Education Research: Vol. 1, Article 5. Available at: https://scholarworks.harding.edu/jger/vol1/iss1/5

Wynn, S. (2006). *Principal leadership, school climate critical to retaining beginning teachers.* Retrieved January 28, 2007 from Duke University Website: http://www.dukenews.edu/2006/04/retention.html.

Zeichner, K.M. (2003). The adequacies and inadequacies of three current strategies to recruit, prepare, and retain the best teachers for all students. *Teachers College Record*, 105(3), 490-519.

Made in United States
Troutdale, OR
02/01/2025